D1525030

PORTUGAL TRAVEL GUIDE 2022

Best Things to See, Do, and Eat!

Explore to Win

TABLE OF CONTENTS

Complete Portuguese Phrasebook
+ Portugal Travel Map

Scan QR code above to claim your free bonuses!

—— OR ——

visit exploretowin.com/portugalbonus

Ready to Sound Like a Portugal Local?

Inside this beginner-friendly Portuguese Phrasebook you'll discover:

- ✓ **Common Words and Phrases:** Quickly learn the local lingo so you can navigate with ease without spending months studying

- ✓ **Pronunciation guides:** Avoid sounding like a foreigner and mix in with the locals effortlessly even if you've never conversed in Portuguese before

- ✓ **Portugal Map:** Access to your exclusive map containing all the major highways, top attractions, and natural sites mentioned in the guide

Scan QR code above to claim your free bonus!

—— OR ——

visit exploretowin.com/portugalbonus

INTRODUCTION

This book is a guide to traveling through Portugal, and it will provide you with all you need to know about the country and what it has to offer before you even take off for your holiday. When planning a trip abroad, knowing as much as you can and remaining optimistic are essential to having an enjoyable and carefree holiday. You want to be informed but also have a positive attitude like any holidaymaker would have. This guide will not only give you insight into traveling as a tourist across the country, but it will also give you the necessary information about what moving to or retiring in Portugal could mean for you. This guide can be useful for all sorts of travelers and anyone who is yearning to explore the many places and spaces of Portugal.

In Chapter 1, we will break down all the necessary travel preparation and admin that come with planning a trip abroad. Here, we will discuss how you can create your very own itinerary that will be perfectly tailored for you and your travel preferences. We will also provide some tips and money-saving hacks to help you create and then stick to a budget. Following a budget will ensure that you do not end your holiday on a low note but rather have consistent fun without worrying about money or how you are going to pay your bills when you get back home. Sticking to a flexible itinerary and a modest budget can help you feel less overwhelmed so that you don't have to think so much on holiday but rather enjoy each day in Portugal.

From here, we will look at some popular tourist destinations and attractions that many travelers visit when in Portugal. If you are the curious type, we have a list of local secrets for you in Chapter 2. In this chapter, we will give you an idea of some places you can visit that showcase the special history and natural beauty of this country. This chapter will cover attractions for all types of travelers to help you decide what kind of traveler you want to be in Portugal. Whether you are wanting a holiday full of outdoor fun or maybe you are interested in architecture and history, we have got you covered!

Chapter 3 will include lists of some great budget-friendly eateries and fine-dining experiences you could try out on your holiday. This chapter will also give you an idea of some accommodations where you could stay on your trip, with a list of different types of accommodations like luxury hotels, budget hostels, and even homestays. We have done our research and found it all for you, so you will just need to choose which accommodation best suits your needs, budget, and travel activities.

In Chapter 4, we will discuss the ins and outs of living in Portugal. This chapter will include lists of the pros and cons of moving to Portugal. The country has seen a rise in expats settling down in its many cities and villages, especially people who are in the retirement stage of their lives. Due to its natural beauty, convenient living, and welcoming atmosphere, many people from all over the world make Portugal their location for their forever home. Not only do people retire in the country, but there is also an opportunity for younger people to live in the country who are not employed by Portuguese businesses. These people are what we call "digital nomads," and Portugal has become a popular destination for those who want to live an adventurous life while working remotely online. All you need is a laptop, a passport, and this guide, and you will be good to go!

Chapter 5 will look at the recent policies related to the Covid-19 pandemic. All countries have created their own policies on how to manage the spread and serious effects of the virus. Portugal has protocols that people need to follow when in the country, but there are also travel policies that have been implemented and these will ultimately affect your travels across the country. Therefore, this guide will give you an update on the Covid-19 protocols of Portugal as well as the recent international travel policies that have been implement-ted in the country concerning tourists and those who are essential travelers.

Lastly, in Chapter 6, we will look at some of the special places and areas to visit in Portugal. Here, we will go through some more hidden and quaint villages. We will also provide some lists of unique Portuguese experiences like festivals and tours that take place in the various regions of the country. Portugal is known for its local wine, and this chapter will give you an idea of the regions to visit if you are seeking a wine country getaway. This chapter will also reveal just how special the country of Portugal is, with its charm felt wherever you go—around its bustling cities, old village streets, and natural landscapes of blue waters and green hills. Portugal has so much to offer, and you will learn everything there is to an authentic Portuguese adventure!

CHAPTER 1:

PLANNING FOR PORTUGAL

Create an Itinerary

Before you can even step onto the plane and leave for your Portuguese destination, you need to know what you would like to do and see when visiting the country. Creating a rough plan or some sort of itinerary will help you move forward on your journey of adventure with little to no stress and complications. A holiday is meant to be enjoyed—why would you want to run into any trouble or delays?

You deserve the best holiday, and this means that you need to *plan* the best holiday. There are a few steps you need to take before you leave for Portugal.

1. Decide on how long you would like your trip to be, and also consider how long you are able to stay. This means that you need to take into account the number of vacation days you are

allowed to have from your work as well as how much time and money you would like to spend in the country. This will also set you up for decision-making and will give you the opportunity to think about what you are willing to compromise on and what you will not compromise on.

2. Create your list of destinations or your travel wishlist. This list does not need to be set in stone, but it will give you an idea of what your true expectations are of your holiday. Your list can be extensive or short, but remember to do some research on the attractions and places you would like to visit as you create this list. This will help you get a clearer idea of what you really can and want to do on your holiday.

3. Create a budget. This budget needs to be as realistic as possible and also needs to leave room for the unforeseen costs that will add up on your trip. We can never have an exact number in our heads, but we can be honest with ourselves when it comes to budgeting for a trip abroad. Remember, this trip is a luxury, and you deserve to be treated to a once-in-a-lifetime holiday experience.

4. Get your documentation together. This includes passports, visas, and other required documents

for travel. Depending on your type of passport, you may not need a visa for Portugal, but always check official sites to make sure you have or can get the correct documentation before you leave. Sometimes waiting for a visa can take a while, so be sure to give yourself enough time to do all this admin. Applying for a passport, if you do not have one already, also includes a waiting period and specific documentation for the application process.

5. Make bookings. These bookings will usually include flights and accommodation. This is why knowing your length of stay is so important. When you book your flights, you may want to book return tickets, which means you have to be certain of the dates you will leave for and return from Portugal. Booking accommodation will also depend on your timeline as well as your travel wishlist. If you have a few activities and attractions in mind, you would want to stay near those specific places. You should also make sure that these bookings will allow you to stick to the budget you made and will give you enough leeway to spend money on activities, food, transportation, and miscellaneous expenses when you are in Portugal. Making some bookings online using apps could save you time

and money. You can look for specials that are on offer to save you some money, while booking some activities that require reservations can definitely save you time.

6. Choose your mode of transportation. This can include different forms, but you would need to do some research on what public transportation services there are in the regions in which you will be staying and also look at the prices of these. To save money, walking is the best "mode of transport," but sometimes the attractions you visit could be far away; therefore, making use of a taxi service, bus, or a rental would be more convenient and smart for saving time. Remember, most services of convenience usually come at a cost, so your mode of transport would also have to be included in your budget. The best way to make your decision is to know your priorities. Do you want to save time? Do you want to save money? Do you want to be in control of your routes and movement? Depending on your travel wish list, your preferences, and your pocket, you would need to decide what your go-to transportation will be. Sometimes, you may have no choice in the matter due to limited transportation services. Whatever you choose, make sure that

it will serve your best interests and only make your trip easier and stress-free.

7. Consider how you will stay connected. Most places have WiFi, but when you are on the go, an internet connection might not always be available to you. Your connection could also be bad or unstable as you travel to different places; this is common when you travel to more isolated places. The most convenient and smart choice would be to get a local SIM card to use throughout the duration of your trip. This will prevent you from getting stuck and only relying on restaurant or accommodation WiFi when you are out and about. Having a local SIM card will also be a better option when it comes to saving money as you will be paying local rates for calls, data, and messages instead of running up your current phone bill with international use.

8. Have yourself covered. Travel insurance is a smart choice when traveling abroad or to a country that you have never been to before. This is because you can never be certain of the problems you may face when traveling across the globe to a foreign country. There are many insurance packages that cover different things, so you need to think about what you view as

important. From baggage to hospital coverage, there is travel insurance for anything at this point. Again, choosing insurance needs to fall in line with your travel wish list, your priorities, as well as your budget. Travel insurance is a great way to ensure that you do not leave a foreign country with additional expenses or run into issues that may leave you stranded, only making your trip less fun. No matter what you choose to do, make sure that your choice is in you and your travel companions' best interests.

9. Do your research on the culture and language. This step is very important if you want to have a rich cultural experience in a foreign country. You do not need to know everything about the history of the place, but knowing a few facts about the city you are staying in or Portuguese customs will help you throughout your trip. Learning a few helpful phrases will make your trip easier. This means learning how to say "please" and "thank you," a few greetings, and a few key questions like "How much does this cost?" or "Where is this building?" will make your life in Portugal much less confusing and overwhelming.

10. Plan and pack. You can plan what you would like to take with you and what you will not

need or use on your trip. This step depends on the length of your stay as well as the time of year that you will be traveling. If you are traveling in summer, you'll want to pack light and loose-fitting clothes. To pack too many close-toed shoes on a summer vacation is not wise as they will take up space and add to the weight of your bag. You may be looking forward to doing some hiking trails, so this would be when packing a pair of close-toed hiking shoes would be necessary. How and what you pack will also be determined by your travel wish list and the types of activities you are planning to take part in. In this way, you will not be wasting time and suitcase space on items that will not end up being used. You also want to not forget important items, but again, you can easily purchase items from local stores that will be much more suitable for the culture and climate of your destination than your current possessions and clothes.

Stick to a Budget

As we know, creating a budget is important when traveling, unless money is no problem for you. Most of us travelers need to save money and allocate certain amounts to necessary travel expenses and specific activities. It is not difficult to create a budget—the challenge comes when you need to stick to it while you are trying to live freely on your holiday abroad. Below is a list of expenses you will need to cover and budget for when planning your holiday:

- Plane tickets
- Visas and other admin or processing fees for required documentation
- Travel insurance
- Accomodation
- Travel gear, kits, and specific clothes
- Transport to and from the airport as well as around the country
- Technology and communication fees and payments like a local SIM card or adaptors
- Food and groceries, including restaurant bills, snacks, groceries, drinks, etc.
- Entrance fees to places like museums and exhibitions
- Excursions and tours
- Miscellaneous items like gifts, clothes, and other special or unforeseen expenses

Now that we have an idea of the many factors that will directly impact your budget, we also need to think of ways you could save money and prevent overspending.

You may want to give yourself time to think about your priorities. You need to ask yourself whether you would rather spend your money on something special, like a unique Portuguese experience, instead of an item you already have at home. Here are some tricks you can follow to save money on holiday:

- Look for deals and sales. This can include deals on flights to weekly restaurant promotions. Remember to keep an eye out for specials, specifically for activities and purchases that you would need to spend money on. You need to prevent spending money on things that are on sale just for the sake of getting these on sale. Always think about what you need to spend money on or the items and experiences you would like to have.

- Try avoiding peak season travel. During the peak holiday season, specifically summer, the prices of almost everything tourist-related are doubled due to higher demand in these months. If you are wanting to save money and the season does not bother you, you could opt for a spring or autumn holiday. Another way to prevent spending your money on inflated prices is to book in advance for flights and for some travel experiences.

- Look for budget-friendly accommodation like hostels or homestays/house-sitting. Remaining flexible with your accommodation will definetely save you money. While some people cannot bear to live outside of a hotel, other travelers who are content with a bed and a shower can find some great deals. You should not compromise your comfort and safety, so be cautious when it comes to going for deals and under-budget accommodations.

- Spend less on transport by walking or taking public transport. Taxi fare and rental cars are much more costly than public transport that locals use every day. Other than using public transport, you can also choose to walk to places, which will give you the opportunity to really immerse yourself in the Portuguese culture on your way to your destination. Remember that you should be wise when it comes to timing as walking takes longer than traveling by car. Therefore, if you need to save time and get to a place sooner, take a bus or make use of a lift app to make your life easier and to prevent wasting precious time during your limited holiday.

- Book activities beforehand. This will save you time and could save you money. Some activities or travel purchases can go up in price the longer you wait to book for your date. Another advantage of booking beforehand is that you can avoid spending money on additional costs that you were not prepared for. You need to keep an open mind while still being wise about your planning and stick to your travel wishlist.

- Get a local SIM card or use free and safe WiFi. International phone rates are insanely high, and therefore, you would want to avoid using your SIM card with your current service provider when in a foreign country. This is why using a local service provider offering cheaper rates is an inevitable money-saver. You can also make use of the WiFi at the accommodation you are staying at or one of your favorite local coffee shops, but just make sure that these are safe and not open to the public without passwords.

- Shop local or eat in. While you are on holiday and ultimately a tourist, you can still save money by shopping like a local. Look out for the stores and stalls that are crowded with locals and opt for grocery shopping over eating out at a restaurant for most meals. If your accommodation has a place for you to cook at home, why not? You could also order takeaway or some ready meals at delis, budget eateries, or grocery stores that are popular among locals.

- Go to free attractions like beaches or hiking trails. Portugal is known for its natural beauty, so there are many free or low-cost attractions you can visit. There are stunning beaches in most regions that are absolutely free. While there are some activities like kayaking or boating that would require fees, you do have many options available to you to compare prices. Some national parks or museums will have entrance fees, but again, look for the ones you really want to go to and also choose some places with lower fees that are not so crowded with tourists. This trick will save you money and time as you will be free of spending your precious holiday time in a long line.

- Avoid paying for too many drinks at bars and restaurants. We all know that beverages are overpriced in most restaurants across the globe, so depending on what you are wanting to drink, you could always opt for something on the lower end of the menu like a large bottle of water. Splitting bottles among your travel companions will save you money as paying per glass for water or wine always winds up being more expensive. See drinking at bars as a treat and not an essential part of your holiday. You could also buy large bottles of water and beverages, even alcoholic beverages, at a grocery store and plan your own picnic or dinner at the beach, park, or at your accommodation.

- Avoid impulsive buying. When on holiday in a foreign place, everything seems new and intriguing, but you need to ask yourself whether the items you see are what you truly need and if you will want it in the future. Gifts to take home are always special, but you do not need to be extravagant with buying local produce or clothing items. Always remind yourself about the limited space in your suitcase as a trick to avoid the temptation of buying unnecessary items.

- Use cash and stick to a daily cash budget. When you can easily just swipe your card without seeing the money leave your hands, it is more likely that you will overspend. Drawing money and having cash on you will remind you of the actual money that you are giving away with every purchase. This is a mental trick to help you stick to your budget. Having cash in Portugal is actually a must as many establishments only take cash as payments, so always carry enough cash on you for your daily outings.

- Get advice from locals. The local people know how to live comfortably in the cities and towns of Portugal. They know the local secrets and the places to go to that are not overpriced tourist traps. Following in the footsteps of the locals when it comes to spending is a smart move as they know the ins and outs of Portuguese life as well as the huge difference between tourist living and modest local living.

CHAPTER 2:

PLACES TO EXPLORE

Best Places to Visit

Top Sights and Attractions

- Mosteiro dos Jerónimos, Lisbon—a monument built to commemorate Vasco da Gama's voyage to India in 1498. The building symbolizes the expansion and power of Portugal in the era of King Manuel and the Portuguese nation between the 15th and 16th centuries. The monument is made up of a church and a monastery and is admired by locals and tourists alike. The exterior and interior of the construc-tion display Manueline architecture with embellishments and breathtaking structures. The tombs of great Portuguese leaders and idols are found in the Mosteiro dos Jerónimos, including, of course, the tomb of explorer Vasco da Gama.

- Torre de Belém, Lisbon—another iconic monu-ment that symbolizes the Portuguese Age of Discovery from the 15th to the 16th century. This tower, which was completed by 1521, was used as a fortress. It showcases the military and patriotic design created by the architect Francisco de Arruda, following the movement of the Manueline period. With stone and mari-time structures, this tower is a must-see if you are interested in Portuguese history and the strong connection made between the country's architec-ture and its past heroic icons, specifically its soldiers and explorers. Despite the practical use of the building, it is now a UNESCO World Heritage Site.

- Convento do Cristo, Tomar—located in an old riverside town, this castle stands out as a majestic structure of power and design. The building used to serve as the headquarters of the Order of the Knights Templar. Inside, there is the Charola, a Templar church that dates back to the medieval period. The inside of this structure is beautifully decorated with fine materials that showcase the symbolism of its origin story. Another attractive feature of this structure is its Manueline window, designed by Diago de Arruda, which stands out from the rest of the building's contrasting materials.

- Bom Jesus do Monte, Braga—a pilgrimage site that is located in eastern Braga. This religious site stands out from its green backdrop due to its grand white stairway of 116 meters. This construction also is made up of a complex of religious architecture, including its several chapels and detailed sculptures that showcase biblical and mythical figures. The structure is separated into three parts. The first part, as you start your way up, is the Sacred Way with the 14 Stations of the Cross. The second part of the journey within the Bom Jesus do Monte is carved statues that showcase the five senses. Lastly, one can admire the Staircase of the Three Virtues—Faith, Hope, and Charity—as you make your way to the church.

- Silves Castle, Silves—a castle located in the old capital city of Moorish Algarve which dates back to the 12th century. The site was well-known for its academic life as it was once a learning hub for Islamic philosophers, writers, and geographers. The structures of Silves were designed and built with the purpose of protection for all its inhabitants. Used as a fortress for Moorish people, the capital was eventually invaded by Crusaders. Despite its history, the castle still stands tall and strong today. It is iconic, not only for its rich history, but also for its design which includes red sandstone, contrasting with the riverside landscape surrounding it. The best time to visit the castle is during the annual Medieval Festival, which is held in early August, so that you can feel like you have been transported back to a time of cultural pride and unique traditions that cannot be found today.
- MNAA National Museum of Ancient Art, Lisbon—a protected home to prominent Portuguese artists throughout history. The museum has exhibits of middle age and even baroque art pieces that were created by well-known Portuguese artists. There are ancient art pieces like the St. Vincent Panels and the Cross of Dom

Sancho I as well as the Reliquary. While the actual exterior of the museum is as grand as other European museums, it is situated in a stunning location, with views of the River Tagus that can be admired from its mini-garden.

- Livraria Lello, Porto—a bookstore that is grand and full of historical literature and design. The architecture of this building showcases a perfect blend of Gothic, Manueline, and Art Nouveau elements. There are grand carpeted staircases and features that make this library look regal. If you are more interested in stunning historical buildings over books, then this library is for you. Livraria Lello is more of a tourist attraction than a functioning local library, as there is an entrance fee and it is often full of visitors from all over the world.

- Capela dos Ossos, Évora—also known as the Chapel of Bones, this is one of the most strange but popular attractions in the country. Due to there being a lack of space for cemeteries in Évora, the monks of the 16th century decided to move human remains to a chapel, which would be known as the "Bone Chapel," in order to store the deceased as well as decorate the chapel's interior. This chapel of the Gothic

Church of St. Francis is now famous for its unique design, with its interior covered by human bones, about 5,00o skeletons, from floor to ceiling. There are skulls and full skeletons of deceased inhabitants as well as the bones of the monks of the church in special coffins. The chapel is a living symbol of the dead, and the imagery and death-inspired design is seen throughout the structure. The chapel was not intended to scare its visitors, but rather to remind the living of the certainty of death and the beautiful circle of life.

Local Secrets to See

- Insensato Café-Livraria, Tomar—a café and bookstore that is enjoyed by many locals. This newer establishment stands out from many other cafés with its contemporary interior and relaxed feel. The menu is vegetarian and vegan-friendly which caters for more of a younger crowd. You can sit and enjoy a fresh cup of coffee while soft music plays in the background. This is a perfect place to take a breather and escape the many tourist-filled restaurants and attractions.

- Jardim da Estrela and Jardim Botânico, Lisbon—these are two of the most beautiful parks enjoyed by Lisbonites. Sheltered by old trees planted back in the Portuguese colonial period, these parks are oases of green within the built-up city of Lisbon. You can pack a picnic and enjoy the many people and plants from all over the world or stroll through these parks to admire the history of Portugal showcased even in its trees. Some of the plants found in the gardens originate from former Portuguese colonies like India and Brazil. These parks also offer amenities and kiosks that you can make use of whenever you are feeling like a walk in a park with a cup of coffee in hand.

- Praia da Figueirinha, Setúbal — a beach to enjoy the local seafood dish from Setúbal known as *choco frito*. When in Portugal, one needs to enjoy the fresh seafood along its beautiful coastline. This beach is a great spot to experience local living and cuisine. This beach is great for a day out, water activities, and of course the once in a lifetime opportunity to try choco frito — fried cuttlefish flavored with garlic, lemon juice, and wine, covered with a cornflour batter.

- Miradouro de Santa Catarina, Lisbon — a square used as the destination of a popular hangout spot for locals. If you are looking for a more relaxed evening with no long lines and tourist-filled restaurants, you can spend some time enjoying a drink at Miradouro de Santa Catarina with the rest of the Lisbonites looking to wind down after a day at work. Here, you can take in the views of Lisbon and look out at the river. The old-style kiosk in the square sells drinks and snacks so that you can stay and become part of the local crowd taking in the evening energy.

- Conímbriga Roman Ruins — one of the best-preserved Roman cities in Portugal. The ruins are made up of Roman structures that date back to the 1st and 2nd century AD, but these were only unearthed in the 2000s. The city's buildings were destroyed over the years after its prime of the 7th to 9th century, but there are still mosaic floors that have stayed intact as well as some buildings' foundations and evening higher stone walls.

- Preserved Head of Diogo Alves, Lisbon — a strange but too intriguing to miss exhibit at the University of Lisbon. Known as Portugal's 1st serial killer, Diogo Alves was born in 1820 and traveled from Galicia to Lisbon. His life of crime led him to go to trial and finally execution. Today, the anatomical theater of the University in Lisbon keeps the head of Alves in a jar. Why? The timing of his execution coincides with the rise of phrenology, now a pseudoscience, and academics in the 1800s wanted to study how the brain was solely responsible for a person's personality, and the skull could be measured to prove this hypothesis. The theater is not always accessible to the public, but private tours or special access could be arranged to really discover the secrets and stories of Lisbon.

- Mina de São Domingos — the abandoned mine with ruins of old buildings and pools of water can be viewed in the Alentejo region. The mine was operational until it closed down in 1996.

The history of this mine is much richer than you would expect as it was occupied by both Phoenician and Roman rule but was rediscovered in the 19th century and used by the British due to the high demand for copper. Because of the industrial growth in the 19th century, the region's population and infrastructure also grew. A thriving village was built close to the mines with all essential facilities as well as a theater and church. The mine became one of the largest in Europe, and after World War I, it switched from a copper mine to a sulfur mine due to the high demand for sulfuric acid. This change led to many workers falling ill with long-term health conditions while the resources were used up, and the consequence was the abandonment of the mine in the 1960s. Today it is a ghost town with the remnants of pollution of the mining industry seen in its water, soil, and environment. With red pools of water from the iron and acid as well as a historical site created by an old miner's house, this small village is still a place of interest for history-loving tourists.

- Capela do Senhor da Pedra, Arcozelo—an ancient pagan worship site located along the beach of Miramar. This chapel, known as the

Chapel of the Lord of Stone, was originally used as a place for pagans to gather and worship freely but was then reclaimed by Christians in the 17th century. The chapel's design and location make it picture-perfect as it is a seaside construction with old stone, mosaics, and gold-leaf altars. Due to its interesting history and being named the "oldest place of worship" of this region of Portugal, there is an annual festival that commemorates the chapel's pagan origins that lasts three days.

Natural Beauty to Admire

- Praia da Falésia — a stunning beach that is a perfect escape from the tourists that flock to Albufeira's popular resort. This beach offers a space to take all that the ocean and seaside living offers. You can walk along the shore, meditate, people watch, and even try out paragliding off the cliffs nearby. This area is close to where all the life is in Albufeira, but a bit less crowded, which makes it convenient in terms of travel while still offering more of a laid back feel. Praia da Falésia is close to the Faro airport as well as many popular accommodations. Location: Olhos de Água, Albufeira, Algarve.

- Poço da Alagoinha — an adventure that will transport you to a magical forest world. This island offers so many outdoor activities like hiking trails, water sports with its landscape, a waterfall, and ponds. This is a perfect place for nature lovers who are yearning to venture deep into the natural wonders that Portugal has to offer. While it may seem like you have been transported to another country… or world, Poço da Alagoinha is only a 20-minute drive away from the Flores airport, and there are many accommodations available in the surrounding areas. This is also a budget-friendly holiday activity as the island has so many free and natural attractions. Location: Flores Island, Azores.

- Islet of Vila Franca do Campo—this islet is a unique natural attraction that one can admire in the archipelago of Portugal. This attraction is special as it is part of an underwater volcano. There is a small beach with clear waters that is perfect for a refreshing swim. This islet is a taste of paradise and can be found just one kilometer from the coast of Azores. The best place to stay is on the island of São Miguel. There are also other activities in the areas like whale watching and a dolphin tour. Location: São Miguel, Azores.

- Benagil Caves—these iconic caves have been enjoyed by tourists and locals for years. To access this spot, you can travel by boat or kayak to this remote beach with arches made of rock. You can enjoy the waters and environment, admiring the natural beauty displayed by the caves, or you can even go on a boat tour and do some dolphin watching. The best and most convenient place to stay would be in Carvoeiro, which can serve as your base as you adventure around the beaches and enjoy water sports, the sun, and local attractions. Location: Carvoeiro, Algarve.

- Pico do Arieiro—this is a natural beauty made of mountainous landscapes and winding paths through trees and tunnels. If you are looking for a more challenging adventure, hiking Pico do Arieiro is a perfect island activity. Not only is the journey unbelievable, but the views are breathtaking. From your position, you will see the colored hills below. This trip will give you a chance to take in the natural beauty of Madeira from a whole new view, about 1,818 meters high at the peak. This is a special day trip that can be enjoyed with a group of friends if you are ever in Funchal. Location: Funchal, Madeira.

- Peneda-Gerês National Park—just an hour's drive from Porto, bordering Spain, this national park can be found in the green landscape that is experienced in northern Portugal. There are many outdoor activities available, including hiking, kayaking, and guided tours like the Gerês Kayaking tour. You can also plan a self-guided tour from Porto to the national park and pack your bags for a day of adventure as you hike the grounds of this park, or opt for a more relaxed experience with a picnic surrounded by the luscious flora and natural streams. Location: outskirts of Porto, Northern Portugal.

- Plantation of orange trees—there is a region of the Algarve free from build-up tourism buildings and made up of nature reserves, farming, and agricultural areas, as well as plantations. You can enjoy the untouched beauty of the Algarve by taking a trip on a hot air balloon above the plantations and green fields of the region. This is a breathtaking experience as the plantations form shapes from trees that can only be seen from an aerial view. There are tours that are available to book your next trip in the sky. Location: Algarve.

- Ponta da Piedade—this is a tourist favorite as the beach and landscape are difficult to miss. The way to this spot is to travel to the light-house and then take the stairs carved in the cliff, which is already a unique route on its own. When you arrive at the beach, you will be able to enjoy the soft sand and clear waters of the Algarve. This spot is iconic with its landscape of sand, ocean, and rock. There are also great activities available in the area including trails, boat trips, and kayaking if you are looking to spend more time adventuring and less time tanning on the beach. Location: Lagos, Algarve.

CHAPTER 3:

BEST PLACES TO EAT, SLEEP, AND RELAX

Taste Portuguese Flavors

Fine and Fabulous Dining

If you are looking for high-quality and authentic Portuguese food, there are countless established and popular restaurants in the many cities and towns across the country. While it might be a lot to sort through, thankfully we have done this for you. We have compiled a list of the top restaurants in the cities Lisbon, Porto, and Braga as well as some other towns and holiday destinations that offer fine dining and some delicious dishes at reasonable prices.

Lisbon

Our top five restaurants:

- Alma — Cuisine: Contemporary Portuguese; Location: R. Anchieta 15
- Taberna Sal Grosso — Cuisine: Portuguese, Mediterranean; Location: Calçada de Forte 22
- August0 Lisboa — Cuisine: Portuguese, European; Location: R. Santana Marinha 26
- Lumi Rooftop Restaurant & Bar — Cuisine: Bar, Mediterranean, International; Location: R. do Diário de Notícias 142 Bairro Alto
- Prova-Enoteca — Cuisine: Mediterranean, European Location: R. Duarte Pacheco Pereira 9E

Restaurants you need to try out:

- Frade — Cuisine: Contemporary Portuguese; Location: Calçada da Ajuda 14
- Loco — Cuisine: Contemporary European; Location: R. dos Navegantes 53-B
- Invicta Madragoa — Cuisine: Seafood, Mediterranean; Location: R. da Esperanca 140
- Belcanto — Cuisine: Contemporary Portuguese, Seafood; Location: R. Serpa Pinto 10A
- Sala — Cuisine: Mediterranean, European; Location: R. dos Bacalhoeiros 103
- Pigmeu — Cuisine: European Fusion; Location: R. 4 de Infantaria 68
- A Avó Tinha Arroios — Cuisine: Portuguese, Mediterranean; Location: R. Ângela Pito 12/13 Mercado de Arroios
- A Nossa Casa — Cuisine: Brazilian-Portuguese, Vegetarian-Friendly; Location: R. da Atalaia 31
- Versículo do Faia — Cuisine: Seafood, Mediterranean; Location: R. da Barroca 60A Bairro Alto
- Grenache — Cuisine: International, Mediterranean; Location: 12 Pátio de Dom Fradique

Porto

Our top five restaurants:

- Cúmplice Steakhouse & Bar — Cuisine: Steakhouse, European, Bar; Location: R. de Passos Manuel 225
- Paparico — Cuisine: Contemporary European; Location: R. de Costa Cabral 2343
- MUU Steakhouse — Cuisine: Steakhouse, European; Location: R. do Almada 149A
- Tascö — Cuisine: Mediterranean, Portuguese; Location: R. do Almada 151A
- Restaurante Chama — Cuisine: Portuguese, European; Location: R. dos Caldeireiros 111

Restaurants you need to try out:

- Simplex Virtus — Cuisine: Bar, International; Location: R. Doutor Barbosa de Castro 59
- Bota & Bira — Cuisine: Steakhouse, Mediterranean; Location: R. O Comércio do Porto 191
- Morabeza Boavista — Cuisine: African-Portuguese; Location: R. de Nossa Senhora de Fátima 495
- Ribeira Square — Cuisine: Mediterranean, European; Location: Praça Ribeira 16
- Petisqueira Voltaria — Cuisine: Mediterranean, Portuguese; Location: R. Afonso Martins Alho 109

- Brasão Foz—Cuisine: Mediterranean, Portuguese; Location: R. de Gondarém 487
- Oficina dos Rissóis—Cuisine: European Portuguese; Location: Passeio São Lázaro 5A
- Travesso Restaurante & Bar—Cuisine: European-Portuguese, Vegetarian-Friendly; Location: R. da Picaria 16 Baixa
- Farinha—Cuisine: Italian, Pizza; Location: R. Doutor Barbosa de Castro 74
- Meia-Nau Porto—Cuisine: Seafood, European; Location: Travessa de Cedofeita 48

Braga

Our top five restaurants:

- Kartilho—Cuisine: Steakhouse, European; Location: R. Dom Afonso Henriques 36
- Restaurante Esperança Verde—Cuisine: European, Portuguese; Location: Avenida Doutor Artur Soares 312
- Omakase—Cuisine: Japanese, Sushi; Location: R. do Raio 6
- Filho da Mãe—Cuisine: Fusion, European; Location: R. Dom Afonso Henriques 25
- pPlace-Restaurant & Cocktail Bar—Cuisine: European, Portuguese, Bar; Location: R. D. Paio Mendes 89

Restaurants you need to try out:

- Casa de Pasto das Carvalheiras—Cuisine: Mediterranean, Contemporary; Location: R. Dom Afonso Henriques 8
- Amor vive na Cozinha—Cuisine: Contemporary, Health; Location: Praça do Comércio 90
- Pizza D'artista—Cuisine: Italian, Neapolitan; Location: Largo da Soutinha 15
- Méze—Cuisine: Café, European; Location: Praça Conde de Agrolongo 71
- Tábuas, Copos & Outras Cenas—Cuisine: European, Portuguese; Location: R. Dom Gonçalo Pereira 54
- Azeite & Alho—Cuisine: Mediterranean, European; Location: R. Costa Gomes 353
- Restaurante O Jacó—Cuisine: Portuguese, Vegetarian-Friendly; Location: Praceta Padre Diamantino Martins 20 Maximinos
- São Frutuoso—Cuisine: Steakhouse, European; Location: R. Costa Gomes 168
- Velhos Tempos—Cuisine: Mediterranean, Portuguese; Location: R. do Carmo 7
- Dom Augusto Restaurante—Cuisine: European, Portuguese; Location: R. de São Vicente 222

Other Locations

- ILHAkAFFÉ-Food & Wine—Cuisine: International, Mediterranean; Location: Estrada Monumental 306, Ground Floor Hotel Florasol, Funchal, Madeira
- Restaurante Martucci—Cuisine: Italian, Mediterranean; Location: Estrada Monumental 314 B, Funchal, Madeira
- Cris's—Cuisine: French, International; Location: Edifício Tecnoparque Passeio Público Marítimo Sítio da, R. da Quinta Calaça, Funchal, Madeira
- Hoyo Hoyo Sabores de Moçambique—Cuisine: African, Portuguese; Location: R. do Vale da Ajuda 35, Funchal, Madeira
- Al Quimia—Cuisine: Contemporary, Portuguese; Location: EPIC SANA Algarve Hotel, Praia da Falésia, Albufeira
- GALERIA Restaurante—Cuisine: Mediterranean, European; Location: R. de Santa Maria 68, Funchal, Madeira
- Restaurante Informal—Cuisine: Mediterranean, Portuguese; Location: R. Dos Murcas 39, Funchal, Madeira

- Conceito Food Store—Cuisine: Contemporary, Portuguese; Location: R. Pequena Urbanização do Viso. Lote 1, Loja A, Cascais
- Fortaleza do Guincho—Cuisine: Seafood, Mediterranean; Location: Estrada do Guincho 2413, Cascais
- Porto Santa Maria—Cuisine: Seafood, Mediterranean; Location: Estrada do Guincho 1937, Cascais

Budget Meals

For those who want to experience the fresh and flavorful dishes of Portuguese food on a budget, there is no need to worry and start counting your euros.

Portugal is known for its affordable prices and home-made meals that can be enjoyed in taverns and cafés in many regions. Depending on your budget and food preferences, you can find local gems in cities and smaller towns that serve good portions and quality food at affordable prices. All you need to do is follow our lead and look for some great spots provided in our lists that we have compiled just for you.

Lisbon

- A Valenciana — Cuisine: Portuguese Takeaway; Location: R. Marquês de Fronteira 157
- La Bonne Crêpe — Cuisine: French, Fast food; Location: R. Marquesa de Alorna 30A
- Tasco Do Vigário — Cuisine: European, Seafood; Location: R. do Vigário 18
- Landeau Chocolate — Cuisine: Café ; Location: R. das Flores 70
- Jam Club — Cuisine: Bar, Portuguese; Location: Travessa dos Inglesinhos 49
- Churrasqueira da Paz — Cuisine: Barbecue, Mediterranean; Location: R. da Paz 78
- Pizzeria Romano Al Taglio — Cuisine: Italian, Fast Food; Location: R. da Conceição 44 Baxia
- Rose Stupa Restaurant — Cuisine: Indian, International; Location: R. Ponta Delgada 80B

- A Cultura do Hambúrguer—Cuisine: American, International; Location: R. das Salgadeiras 38
- As Bifanas do Afonso—Cuisine: Portuguese, Fast Food; Location: R. da Madalena 146
- Quase Café—Cuisine: International, European, Healthy; Location: R. do Salvador 32
- Eight: The Health Lounge—Cuisine: European, Healthy; Location: Praça da Figueira 12A
- Focaccia in Giro—Cuisine: Italian, Pub; Location: Campo de Santa Clara 141

Porto

- Curb Burgers—Cuisine: American, Fast Food; Location: R. do Belomonte 70
- Árvore do Mundo—Cuisine: European, Healthy; Location: R. Duque Loulé N 228
- Hungry Biker—Cuisine: European, Café; Location: R. das Taipas 68
- Pregar—Cuisine: Portuguese, Bar; Location: Largo São Domingos 96
- LAZY Breakfast Club—Cuisine: International, Vegetarian-Friendly; Location: R. das Oliveiras 110
- Restaurante Cana Verde—Cuisine: Mediterranean, European; Location: R. dos Caldeireiros 121

- Só Tapas—Cuisine: Mediterranean, Portuguese; Location: Largo Maternidade Júlio Dinis 8
- Folias de Baco—Cuisine: Portuguese, Wine Bar; Location: R. dos Caldeireiros 136
- A Sandeira—Cuisine: European, Bar; Location: R. dos Caldeireiros 85
- Gazela Cachorrinhos da Batalha—Cuisine: Portuguese, Bar; Location: Travessa Cimo de Villa 4
- Oficina dos Rissóis—Cuisine: European, Portuguese; Location: Passeio São Lázaro 5A
- Uata?! Porto—Cuisine: Fast Food; Location: R. das Taipas 100
- Confeitaria São Domingos—Cuisine: Café, Portuguese; Location: Largo sé São Domingos 37

Braga

- Tasquinha do Fujacal—Cuisine: Mediterranean, European; Location: Alameda do Fujacal 99
- Petisqueira Confiança—Cuisine: Mediterranean, European; Location: Avenida Padre Júlio Fragata 96

- Bira dos Namorados—Cuisine: European, Diner, Bar; Location: R. Dom Gonçalo Pereira 85
- Capitão Espetada—Cuisine: Brazilian-Portuguese, Barbecue, Bar; Location: Largo 12 de Dezembro 37 Lomar
- Friends Food & Drinks—Cuisine: American-Brazilian, Fast Food; Location: Largo 12 de Dezembro 8
- Maximinense—Cuisine: Pizza, Portuguese; Location: R. de Caires 299
- Restaurante Vegetariano Gosto Superior—Cuisine: European, Healthy; Location: Praça Mouzinho de Albuquerque 29
- Pizzaria Luzzo Braga—Cuisine: Italian, Pizza; Location: Praça Conde de Agrolongo 182
- Dona Petisca—Cuisine: Mediterranean, European; Location: R. Dom Paio Mendes 32
- Sanno: Healthy & Real Food—Cuisine: Café, Healthy; Location: Largo São João do Souto 13A
- Tasca do Carregal—Cuisine: Mediterranean, Portuguese, Vegan-Friendly; Location: Avenida do Carregal 162
- Bicla Burgers—Cuisine: European, Fast Food, Pub; Location: R. Gabriel Pereira de Castro 68

- Aqui Às 5—Cuisine: European, Healthy; Location: R. Quinta de Cabanas 21 São Vicente

Other Locations

- Giro Churros & Paninis—Cuisine: Café, Portuguese; Location: R. Carreira 77, Funchal, Madeira
- Adega Moniz—Cuisine: Mediterranean, Portuguese; Location: R. de S. Pedro 58 Santa Cruz, Gaula, Madeira
- Bar O Ideal—Cuisine: Bar, Seafood; Location: R. do Cais 16, Paul do Mar, Calheta, Madeira
- Restaurante Cantinho do Mar—Cuisine: Mediterranean, Portuguese; Location: Torre da Medronheira Olhos D'Água, Albufeira
- Le Bistrot Jacaranda—Cuisine: French, Mediterranean; Location: 28F Avenida do Infante, Funchal, Madeira
- Beats & Burritos—Cuisine: Mexican, Vegetarian Friendly; Location: Travessa do Cotovelo 4, Lagos
- Bloomy Market—Cuisine: European, Healthy; Location: Avenida Lusia Todi 163, Setubal
- Jukebox Tapas & Meals—Cuisine: Seafood, Mediterranean; Location: R. Soeiro da Costa 40A, Lagos

- Al-Bravo Cafe & Shop—Cuisine: Mediterranean, Contemporary; Location: R. da Extrema 31, Lagos
- Goji Lounge Café—Cuisine: Café, European; Location: R. Marreiros Netto N 61, Lagos
- Poké Lagos—Cuisine: Healthy, Hawaiian; Location: R. Dom Vasco da Gama 12A, Lagos
- Beco Da Ribeira—Cuisine: Bar, European; Location: Beco da Ribeira 4, Setúbal
- Rusty'co Bar & Restaurante—Cuisine: Bar, Contemporary; Location: Estrada de Santa Eulália Loja AC, Albufeira

Where to Stay

Luxury Living

When on holiday, we often want to live a different life and spoil ourselves with the best of the best. If you are one of those people who want to experience a regal and luxurious holiday, then you need to stay at one of the fine hotels we have found. We have compiled a list of some of the top luxury stays in Portugal, specifically in the cities of Lisbon, Porto, and Braga, as well as some other popular holiday locations like the Algarve and Madeira.

Lisbon

- VIP Executive Picoas Hotel — Location: R. Filipe Folque 12; Price: €70
- Corpo Santo Lisbon Historical Hotel — Location: Largo do Corpo Santo 25; Price: €190
- Wine & Books Lisboa Hotel — Location: Travessa da Memória 56; Price: €160
- TURIM Boulevard Hotel — Location: Avenida da Liberdade 159, Santo Antônio; Price: €227
- Hotel Real Palacio — Location: R. Tomás Ribeiro 115, Avenidas Novas; Price: €128
- TURIM Saldanha Hotel — Location: R. Pedro Nunes 16, Avenidas Novas; Price: €131

Porto

- Vincci Porto—Location: R. Alameda Basílio Teles 26/33, Lordelo do Ouro e Massarelos; Price: €74
- Casual Inca Porto—Location: Praça Coronel Pacheco, 52, União de Freguesias do Centro; Price: €70
- ABC Hotel Porto-Boavista—Location: União de Freguesias do Centro; Price: €70
- Vera Cruz Porto Downtown Hotel—Location: R. Ramalho Ortigão, 14, União de Freguesias do Centro; Price: €136
- Porto Palácio Hotel—Location: Avenida da Boavista, 1269, Lordelo do Ouro e Massarelos; Price: €167
- Torel Avantgarde—Location: 336 R. da Restauração, União de Freguesias do Centro; Price: €224

Braga

- The Arch-Charming Apartments in the Historic Center—Location: R. Dom Diogo de Sousa 51; Price: €72
- Melia Braga Hotel & Spa—Location: Avenida General Carrilho da Silva Pinto; Price: €110

- Urban Hotel Estação—Location: Largo da Estação 13; Price: €58
- Hotel Villa Garden Braga—Location: Largo de Infias - São Vicente; Price: €71
- Vila Gale Collection Braga—Location: Largo Carlos Amarante; Price: €173
- Hotel do Parque—Location: Monte do Bom Jesus; Price: €133

Other Locations

- Pestana Churchill Bay—Location: R. Nossa Senhora da Conceição, 9000–113 Câmara de Lobos; Price: €147
- Hotel Quinta Do Furao—Location: Achada Do Gramacho, 9230–082 Santana; Price: €137
- Hotel Marina Rio—Location: Avenida Dos Descobrimentos, S/N, 8600–645 Lagos; Price: €90
- Grand Muthu Forte do Vale—Location: R. Dunfermline, 8200–278 Albufeira; Price: €118
- Vila Algarvia Boutique & Suites—Location: Travessa Primeiro de Dezembro 7, Albufeira City Centre, 8200–207 Albufeira; Price: €80
- Grande Real Santa Eulália Resort & Hotel Spa—Location: Estrada de Albufeira - Olhos d'água, 8200–269 Albufeira; Price: €159

Budget Stays

Some of us, when traveling abroad, would rather choose to spend our money and time on outdoor and unique adventures than stay at a luxury hotel. This is why it is important to know what kind of budget stays are available in the city you are planning to travel in. The cities of Portugal and the many popular tourist towns offer a variety of accommodations that range in price. You will be surprised at how much money you can save by staying at a hostel or a budget hotel, which would give you more leeway to spend money on tours and fun activities.

Lisbon

- B & B Hotel Lisboa Aeroporto—Location: R. Vasco da Gama 5; Price: €57
- Hotel Alif Campo Pequeno—Location: Av. João XXI 80, Campo Pequeno, Areeiro; Price: €56
- Avenue Rooms & Suites—Location: R. Rodrigues Sampaio 138, Santo Antônio; Price: €34
- Green Heart Hostel—Location: R. Santa Marta 37, Santo Antonio; Price: €12-36
- Apartments Center Alfama—Location: R. de São João da Praça 51, Santa Maria Maior; Price: €56

- Silk Lisbon — Location: R. Tomás Ribeiro 40, 2 Esq, Avenidas Novas; Price: : €63

Porto

- Garden in Town Hostel — Location: Região Norte, R. da Alegria 1000, Bonfim; Price: €29
- Star Inn Porto — Location: R. Senhora Do Porto 930, Ramalde; Price: €53
- Hotel América — Location: R. de Santa Catarina 1018, Bonfim; Price: €48
- Pao de Acucar Hotel — Location: R. do Almada 262, União de Freguesias do Centro; Price: €49
- Hotel Peninsular — Location: R. Sá da Bandeira 21, União de Freguesias do Centro; Price: €34
- Boavista Class Inn — Location: Avenida da Boavista 621, Lordelo do Ouro e Massarelos; Price: €61

Braga

- Flag Hotel Braga — Location: R. Damiana Maria Da Silva; Price: €38
- InBraga Hostel — Location: R. da Boavista 21; Price: €15
- Golden Tulip Braga Hotel — Location: Estrada Via Falperra, Santa Cristina de Longos, Nogueira; Price: €52

- B&B Hotel Braga Lamacaes — Location: Av. D. João II 75; Price: €52
- Hotel Senhora a Branca — Location: Largo da Senhora A Branca 58; Price: €55
- Habitar Guest House — Location: Avenida da Liberdade 33; Price: €41

Other Locations

- Dorisol Mimosa Studio Hotel — Location: R. da Casa Branca, São Martinho, 9004–535 Funchal; Price: €56
- Dom Pedro Lagos — Location: Pinhal da Meia Praia, 8600–315 Lagos; Price: €54
- Bura Surfhouse — Location: R. da Pedra Alçada 15, 8600–546 Lagos; Price: €15-36
- Olive Hostel Lagos — Location: R. da Oliveira 67, 8600–700 Lagos; Price: €17-44
- Grand Muthu Forte do Vale — Location: R. Dunfermline, 8200-278 Albufeira; Price: €57
- Alte Hotel — Location: Estrada de Sta. Margarida, Montinho, 8100–012 Alte; Price: €48

Local Homestays

The Portuguese culture is rare and offers a unique way of life that cannot be experienced fully from a week in a tourist-dominated town. If you are curious about the Portuguese lifestyle and want to experience a more authentic stay in the country, you could find a local home to make as your holiday accommodation. Choosing to live in a homestay will also give you some insight into local living and Portuguese suburbs, which could be helpful if you are planning to move or retire in Portugal in the near future.

Lisbon

- Be Lisbon Residence Marquês—Location: Avenida António Augusto de Aguiar 56, 1 esq, Avenidas Novas; Price: €46
- The Tram 18 Space—Location: R. Aliança Operária 95, 1 esq, Ajuda; Price: €20
- Quarto suite em Belém—Location: Rua do Galvão 29, 3 Andar, Belém; Price: €50
- D&N Hospedagem-Almirante—Location: Avenida Almirante Reis 136, Arroios; Price: €36
- Ledi's Housing—Location: 6 R. Quirino da Fonseca, R. Quirino da Fonseca 6, 3 Direito, Arroios; Price: €48
- Theorynomad Rooms AL Lisboa—Location: Av. Óscar Monteiro Torres, 20A, Porta 2i, Areeiro; Price: €42

Porto

- Casa do Sol—Location: R. de João Pedro Ribeiro 673, 1o, União de Freguesias do Centro; Price: €50
- Lolla's City House—Location: R. de Júlio Dinis 891, Lordelo do Ouro e Massarelos; Price: €37
- Hostel Brazuca—Location: 292 Travessa de Nova Sintra, Campanhã; Price: €37
- ChatNoir Porto LaMaison—Location: R. de Brito Capelo 51, União de Freguesias do Centro; Price: €42
- Astronaut Rooms—Location: R. do Morgado de Mateus 183, 2 andar, Bonfim; Price: €33
- AL-Almada 4—Location: R. do Almada 332, 4, União de Freguesias do Centro; Price: €39

Braga

- Casa de Guadalupe—Location: R. de Guadalupe 71; Price: €104
- Quinta dos Campos-Apartamento 1—Location: R. dos Campos 49; Price: €58
- Enjoy Braga Estação—Location: R. Moura Coutinho 48, 3EQ; Price: €43
- Quinta do Gestal—Location: Avenida do Casal 50, 4730-575 Casal; Price: €81
- Lux Housing Século XXI—Location: Largo Sra. A. Branca 126; Price: €187

Other Locations

- Dazk Golden Estate — Location: Estrada de São João 28, Sítio do Barreiro, 9350–103 Ribeira Brava; Price: €61
- Resort Room Fazenda Viegas — Location: Estrada da Atalaia s/n, 8600–281 Lagos; Price: €88
- Sleep Inn Guest House — Location: Rua Marreiros Neto 54, 3A, 8600–754 Lagos; Price: €64
- Residencial Família — Location: Sítio Pé da Ladeira-Caminho do Cemitério 24, 9200–088 Machico; Price: €58
- Villa Monaco — Location: R. batista severino lote 104 MONTENEGRO, 8005–237 Faro; Price: €75
- Heaven's Edge — Location: São Brás de Alportel, 8150–128 São Brás de Alportel; Price: €69

CHAPTER 4:

LIVING AND RETIRING IN PORTUGAL

Expat Living in Portugal

Not only is Portugal a great holiday destination, but it has become a sought after place to move to or even retire for a long-term period. Many people have taken the leap and packed up for Portugal. Expat living is quite popular in Portugal and people choose to buy a property or have long-term rentals in order to live in the country as a local. Many people have chosen to make Portugal their new home, so if you are one of the people who is wanting to make the move, this chapter will help give you the information and tips you will need to make the best decision for you and your family. Whether you are planning to retire or stay in the country for a year or two as a younger digital nomad, we will look at the steps and factors involved in the move.

Best Places to Live

Before you make the move or get the ball rolling with immigration documentation, you need to think about what you would like and your ideal lifestyle. This means that you need to take a moment to really think about your needs and wants in your current living situation as well as your potential future Portuguese life. Here, you would look at where you would prefer to live. Are you more of a coastal person or a city person? What will your income be like? What area would you be able to afford to live in? Are you needing to be close to amenities or would you prefer to be situated in a more isolated, rural area? These are a few questions you need to ask yourself and answer truthfully before you take action.

While you focus on your Portuguese dream, we have you covered with the location. Below is a list of places that are ideal for living as an expat in Portugal:

- Lisbon. This is the capital city of Portugal, and due to this fact, it offers all you can really ask for in a European city. With the natural beauty and all the conveniences of a big city, Lisbon is a perfect place to set up your new home. This city is unique due to its distinct Portuguese flair that has merged with more contemporary living. This means you can enjoy the culture inherent to this country while also enjoying more universal amenities and activities. The downside to living here would be that it is a tourist hub, meaning that prices are higher than other cities or regions of Portugal. The diversity does make the extra money spent worth it, especially if this kind of city lifestyle is what you truly desire. Another plus to living here would be the good public transport and the abundance of local services and markets that still thrive in a city that is full of tourists. Lisbon can definitely be your new home.

- Porto. The second largest city in Portugal offers so much choice and freedom when it comes to settling in the country. It is located in northern Portugal along the Douro River and really does provide so much local culture, amenities of a city, as well as natural beauty. Porto holds a World Heritage Site as it is rich in Portuguese history that has been preserved over decades. Due to the attractions of this region, there can be a flood of tourists in the city center, but you can definitely find quieter areas that are perfect for settling down located on the outskirts of the center. Not only can you enjoy the nature, peace, and quiet in these surrounding areas, but you will also benefit from the lower property prices of homes just outside the city center.

There is a home for everyone, from apartments to larger villas and family homes. Due to the convenience and affordable prices in this region, it has grown to be popular among expats. Some areas that have been favorable for expats include Vila Nova da Gaia, Madelena, Lavadores, Campanha, Ribeira, Ramalde, and the more affluent area of Foz do Douro.

- Braga. This is another large city in the north of Portugal, other than the capital, which provides the amenities of city life as well as some rich history and authentic Portuguese living. Braga is the third-largest city in the country and therefore offers old buildings rich in Portuguese history and architecture. There are several landmarks and tourist attractions that showcase the heritage of this city, but this is contrasted with the construction of the modern architecture of newer buildings. Most properties in the city center are not accessible or on sale, so many expats and new homeowners lean towards properties on the outskirts like in the northern quarter or closer to the university. Not only do these locations offer more of a laid-back and quieter lifestyle, but their prices are also much more affordable. Due to the age of the city, many buildings require repair; therefore, if you are seeking an authentic Portuguese life in Braga, be sure to get your hands dirty and be open to renovation to create your forever home.

- Aveiro. Known as the "Venice of Portugal" and located in central Portugal, Aveiro is an ideal place to settle in. With stunning canals and historical buildings, this city is a true-Portuguese city. Despite all it has to offer, the city does receive fewer tourists than other cities in Portugal, which makes it a much more comfortable place to live for expats and retirees. The city has expanded its development and there are more apartments and residential areas. For a more affordable and quieter city, Aveiro is the place for you. Its location is also perfect for commuting to bigger cities like Lisbon and Porto if you are ever keen to get in on the action of big city activities.

- Chaves. Close to the southern Spanish border, this town is quaint with stunning old-world architecture with a backdrop of nature's beauty. Chaves is rural and makes for a more quiet, yet authentic Portuguese life. This town is for relaxing and enjoying the peace provided by small-town living, which is perfect for digital nomads who need an escape from city life or travel bloggers. This town is also great for retirees, with affordable housing and a laid-back lifestyle in a friendly community.

- Coimbra. Situated between Lisbon and Porto, this city is convenient in so many ways. There is a university as well as many property investment opportunities. Whether you are planning to retire—which Coimbra is an inviting place for retirees—or a young adult wanting to study or work in a lovely Portuguese city, this is the place to be. While the property in the city center and close to the university are sought after and sold at a higher price, you can easily buy a property just outside these areas for an affordable price. Coimbra offers a convenient and high quality of living while having lower costs when it comes to expenses, especially housing costs. There is an array of older houses that just need a bit of TLC that one can easily buy at a bargain.
- The Algarve. This region is a popular tourist destination as it offers holidaymakers pristine beaches and an authentic holiday vibe. There are many hotels as well as local communities. Its tourism industry is the main reason why many foreign investors purchase property in the Algarve, but this region is also great for expats and retirees. You have options to live in

central Algarve, the port of Portimão, or even the more affordable city of Faro. Depending on your wants, needs, and budget, you can definitely live out your seaside dreams when living in the Algarve as it has so many property and lifestyle options available.

- Setúbal. This port city is close to Lisbon and is loved by both tourists and expats. This is because it is located right on the water and it also has a thriving fishing and wine industry. There are also many local attractions and quaint areas to explore. One can purchase a property here for a reasonable price and still enjoy all the perks of living along the coastline and experiencing beach life. The further you travel out of the city and away from the port, the cheaper the property becomes, so if you are on a budget you can still afford your dream home in this seaside city for a good deal.

- Madeira Archipelago. The islands of Madeira offer laid-back island living at affordable prices. Not only is this a great option for retirees, but it is also a great holiday destination if you are ever looking for a unique Portuguese experience. Due to its location between Lisbon and the African coastline, the islands of Madeira bring their own culture and take on Portuguese flair.

The archipelago consists of two inhabited islands out of the seven and two isles—the islands of Madeira, Porto Santo and Desertas. While space may be an issue, there are still property investment opportunities due to the archipelago's tourism industry and its exotic location.

Cost of Living

The cost of living in Portugal is relatively low and quite affordable for the middle-class. While there are opportunities for you to live in luxury in the country, it is welcoming to those who are looking for an easy, holiday-all-year-round lifestyle at a lower price than other European countries. Let us break down the average cost of living in Portugal. A monthly budget of €2000 for two people, including expenses like rent for a one-bedroom apartment, groceries, water, electricity, gas and heating, a phone line, internet, cable TV, as well as leisure items or experiences like eating can come to just under the monthly budget, around €1,750. This means that a single person can live comfortably with a budget of €1000. Of course, if you are more of a spender and want to live right on the beach or in a sought-after area, you would find yourself spending more on rent, but this just goes to show that Portugal offers much variety and you are spoiled for choice when moving to this country.

In the big cities like Lisbon and Porto, you will spend more on rent per month due to the occupation of space and the higher demand for properties in these regions. If you are looking for a quieter place to settle down, then you will spend less on rent or even on your purchase of land. The other aspect of living in a city is that the cost of living is higher than in more rural areas or smaller towns. While there are tourist hotspots outside of the cities that can have higher-priced properties, it is very easy to avoid tourist prices in these towns. Before you can decide where you would like to live, you need to weigh up all your options and know your true desires and dreams as well as some practical steps involved in making your move to Portugal.

The Pros and Cons of Living in Portugal

Pros of Living in Portugal	Cons of Living in Portugal
• Affordable living costs for people who are starting out • Safe environment for solo travelers or digital nomads • Friendly people and communities • Lower tax rates • Necessary amenities • Convenience in vibrant cities and towns • Perfect landscapes for outdoor adventures • Pleasant weather • Diverse cultures and people in cities • Relaxing natural beauty	• The need to learn a new language, Portuguese • Carry cash on you at all times due to limited card transaction opportunities • Adjusting to a different climate • The lack of updated appliances and features in older apartment buildings, e.g. no central heating • A much slower pace of life

• Accessible and affordable property for buying or renting • Centrally located and close to other European holiday destinations and tourist attractions • Offers stress-free and laidback living across the country	

Portugal as Your Retirement Destination

Portugal is a popular destination for retirees due to the laid back and convenient lifestyle, and let us not forget about the relaxing natural beauty that surrounds you all the time. There are many factors to consider and even more steps you need to take in terms of documentation and administration procedures. Of course, for EU citizens, retiring in Portugal is hassle-free, and they can simply apply for residency through immigrations services known as Serviço de Estrangeiros e Fronteiras (SEF). EU citizens can visit many of the SEF offices to receive their residency.

For those who are not EU citizens, the process of retirement in Portugal involves the process of getting a residence permit which lasts for five years and then one can apply for residency through the Golden Visa scheme. To get a residency permit, you will need to apply at the closest Portuguese consulate and provide documents such as a valid passport, proof that you have enough funds, health insurance, as well as any criminal record. From here, you can follow the instructions of officials and wait until the processing of documents has been completed. If you want to retire in Portugal and make it your forever home, applying for the Golden Visa scheme, which was implemented in 2012, will allow you to live in the country for as long as you wish through purchasing a property in the country.

The Pros and Cons of Retiring in Portugal

Pros of Retiring in Portugal	Cons of Retiring in Portugal
• Affordable living costs • Lower tax and ease in tax laws and retirement tax • Necessary amenities • Convenience in vibrant cities and towns • Easy retiring laws for	• Non-English speaking • Rundown older buildings in some towns • Small towns and rural areas have fewer amenities and facilities for older people like healthcare and clinics.

EU citizens and non-EU citizens • Pleasant weather • Relaxing natural beauty • Accessible and affordable real estate for foreign investors • Centrally located and close to other European holiday destinations • Access to Portuguese citizenship after five years in the country • Stress-free and laid-back living	

Portuguese Social Norms and Local Lifestyle

Just like every country, Portugal has its distinct social norms, unwritten rules, and traditions. When you move to and choose to live here, you will need to adopt these specific Portuguese ways of living in order to become immersed and accepted in the communities. Some of the very obvious features of Portuguese culture are that people are friendlier and much more welcoming. If you are not used to this, you may find that people are too forward, but this is how people connect with others. People in this country are people-oriented and extremely helpful and hospitable.

Therefore, when you move and become part of a community in Portugal, you would need to become more of a people person while also being supportive of some older, more traditional Portuguese ways of living that may have been forgotten in other cities across the globe. Family, preserving cultural and religious traditions, as well as being open and focused on one's community are all important and central to the Portuguese way of life. Upholding local treasures, industry, and protecting people and the environment are important to the culture of this country. Therefore, socializing and following a more laid-back lifestyle are ways to uphold the ways of life when living in Portugal.

CHAPTER 5:

TRAVELING DURING COVID-19

Traveling to another country will always require some adjustments and planning before leaving, but traveling during a time of a global pandemic requires more preparation. Due to the Covid-19 pandemic, travel, especially international, has become quite restricted. This is not to say that you cannot travel at all, but travel does include extra precautions that were non-existent in the past. In this chapter, we will go through the national protocol and policies of Portugal so that you will be well-equipped and fully prepared for your trip without running into complications like quarantining or extra testing.

Covid-19 Protocol

The nationally accepted behavior during Covid-19 in Portugal is similar to other countries, while there has been an ease in restrictions lately. Due to the pandemic, there have been universal social rules that have been implemented to prevent the spread of the Covid-19 virus, which has directly affected how people socialize. Therefore, some additional social rules that have been created and followed in Portugal to control the virus include

- wearing face masks in closed spaces, especially public spaces.
- social distancing by keeping at least a 1m space between yourself and others.
- washing hands with soap and water regularly, especially after touching objects outside of your own home.
- upholding etiquette of covering your mouth and nose when sneezing or coughing with your elbow.
- sanitizing when entering public establishments.
- wearing face masks and keeping a distance from others when using public transport.

Portuguese Travel 2022 Policies

To protect its citizens and its tourists, Portugal has its own policies that have been implemented with the goal of prevention and management. When it comes to traveling around Portugal as a tourist, the country requires its visitors to follow its guidelines as its law enforcement and citizens follow the policies put forward by the government. There are different guidelines among the regions of Portugal, but most share the same sentiment and policies.

If you are a traveler who will be in mainland Portugal, the region allows essential and non-essential travel across its towns and cities. When it comes to mandatory documentation, vaccination cards, and testing, the process may differ depending on the country you are traveling from. For instance, travelers from the European Union (EU) and Schengen countries can travel freely with proof of an EU digital vaccination card or recent and valid negative Covid-19 test. Non-essential travelers from countries outside of the EU and Schengen nations consist of a shortlist, mainly from the UAE and China as well as some South American countries like Chile, Colombia, and Peru, etc. If you are traveling from a country that is not on this list, your travel would need to be classified as 'essential.' This means that the purpose for your travel to mainland Portugal would need to include study, work, health procedures, or family responsibility.

To travel to Portugal, you would need to be vaccinated by one of a few vaccinations recognized and accepted by the European Medicines Agency, as Portugal is an

EU country. Therefore, popular and verified global vaccines like Pfizer, Moderna, and AstraZeneca are accepted by the Portuguese government.

Before flying to the cities of Portugal, you will be expected to fill out a questionnaire about your current health and Covid-19 related topics. Testing is an additional precaution that is encouraged by all ports and entrances to Portuguese territories. Unlike some larger cities and regions, the islands of Madeira are less strict when it comes to entering the archipelago. In fact, there are no official restrictions for travelers of any sort in the archipelago, yet testing before and after travel is encouraged but not mandatory. The wearing of masks in public places and proof or card of vaccination or a negative Covid-19 test is required when entering social institutions like bars and restaurants.

CHAPTER 6:
SELF-GUIDED TOURS

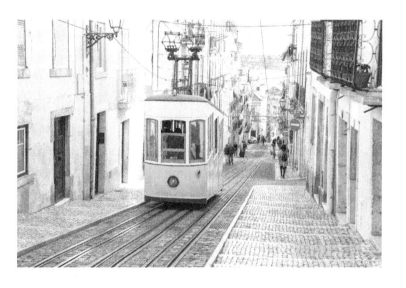

Wander Around Small Towns

Although there are popular cities in Portugal that offer great activities and unforgettable experiences for all visitors, there are also smaller towns that have not been changed due to the booming tourism industry.

Portugal is made up of many old villages and quiet seaside towns that offer authentic Portuguese food, traditions, and unspoiled natural beauties like secret caves and private beaches. There are many magical places to explore waiting for you right outside of the cities. Below is a list of some treasured towns that can be found across the country:

- Parque Nacional da Peneda-Gêres and Sistelo — a village near the national park, "Peneda Gêres" is a tiny settlement of about 300 inhabitants. The village is a national wonder due to its size and preserved history. Sistelo is nicknamed the "little Portuguese Tibet," with hand-made terraces and well-maintained sustainable pastures for grain harvesting, specifically corn along the river. The village has a viewpoint, the "Cha da Armada," and offers stunning views of the green landscape and the whole of Sistelo. For more adventure, one can go on hiking trails.

- Monsanto — a village built around large boulders. This mountaintop village has been named one of the most Portuguese villages in Portugal due to its landscape as well as its historic buildings. There are remains of a Templar castle and all the original houses have been protected for hundreds of years. Monsanto can be viewed as a living museum as it is a village that is still inhabited while preserving the past. One can stroll down the narrow streets and admire the cottages from another time that have been built into rocks that have stood the test of time. The rock structures in this village represent the strength of Portuguese culture and prove just how the history and creations of its people still have relevance today.

- Azenhas do Mar—a small fishing village just outside of Lisbon. The town is picturesque and the bright, contrasting colors of the white houses and blue sea is perfect for a traveling photographer. The town is small enough for you to spend the day on the beach relaxing on the golden sand or taking a refreshing dip in the ocean. There are also local seafood restaurants that will offer you an array of authentic Portuguese cuisine.

- Quinta da Regaleira, Sintra—just north of Lisbon, you can explore the city of Sintra which is known for its beautiful palaces and castles. When you are in this region, you will feel like you have time traveled into a fairytale land from a past era. A must-see is the "Pena Palace" that displays the wealth and opulence of the historical homes of Sinta. Due to its popularity, you should book tickets online before your trip to avoid long lines.

- Berlengas Archipelago, Peniche—this fishing village offers natural beauty as well as unspoiled, authentic Portuguese living. The archipelago of this area is just a 10-minute boat ride from the village of Peniche, and here you can enjoy the old seaside structures and the stunning views from these buildings. There is a lighthouse and a fort on Berlenga Grande, the main island of this archipelago. This archipelago, which holds historic buildings surrounded by precious natural beauty, is part of a nature reserve. The small beach is perfect for a quieter beach day and a relaxing, private experience.

- Santana, North of Madeira—known for its iconic, colorful, triangular houses, this village is another example of a living museum. The houses are unique as they are traditional in design and are now used as souvenir shops, which boosts its tourism industry. Currently, only one of these historical houses is inhabited while the rest of this community is admired by tourists and aspiring photographers who cannot help but capture the rainbow of houses that makes this village stand out. There are also hiking trails in the area that offer more luscious, forestry terrain of northern Portugal.

Unique Experiences

While there are many national parks and exquisite beaches, the people of Portugal also bring life to the cities and villages with festivities and many unique, authentic Portuguese activities. Here, we will go through some festivals that Portuguese people celebrate on a yearly basis while also looking at some tours that you can experience with local guides or on your own. Portugal is rich with history, delicious seafood, natural sight, as well as some rare activities like wine tasting and cruises along its seas and rivers. The adventure is waiting for you…

Festivals

Festivals are central to Portuguese culture and are organized and enjoyed by locals annually. Below is a list of some of the main festivals full of colors, customers, music, and food that you could experience in Portugal:

- Semana Santa, Braga — a week-long Easter celebration that is full of decorations like flowers and bright lights in the streets of Braga city. A street altar is present while men, known as *Farricocos*, dressed in tunics and hoodies walk around the streets.

- Madeira Flower Festival—in the month of May, the streets and clocks of Madeira are covered in flowers, which decorate the city in many colors, displaying the beauty of the flora of Madeira.
- Festas de Lisboa, Lisbon—this festival is an annual celebration of the life of Saint Anthony. The festival lasts for the first week of June until about the 13th of June. The people of the city celebrate by parading along Avenida da Liberdade, which is a procession that honors the Saint. The festivities occur in the city streets, which are filled with food, specifically roasted sardines, music, dancing balloons, and wreaths. Many neighborhoods of Lisbon celebrate this festival and can experience this in the Alfama, Ajuda, Bairro Alto, Mouraria, Graça, as well as the Castle.
- Festas Sanjoaninas, Azores—this celebration occurs during the month of June. It is a very old festival and includes an opening process, queen parade, and even street bull racing.
- Feira de Porto, Porto—this is a celebration that occurs between June 24th and 25th with food,

local wine, dance, and fireworks that can be admired on Rio Douro.

- São Mateus Fair, Viseu—this is a month-long celebration that starts from the beginning of August and goes on until the beginning of September. The festivities occur in the medieval city and people take part in folklore and handicraft, play and dance to music, and enjoy local food to keep the spirits of locals high and proud for the entire month.

Tours and Tasting

- Pastel de Nata Workshop, Lisbon Bakery— there is an opportunity for you to go behind the scenes and discover the process of making the national pastry of Portugal, pastel de nata. You will have the chance to learn how to make your own creamy tarts with the guidance of a professional chef. This is a fun activity that not only teaches you a skill with insight into the famous pastry, but you will also experience traditional food and make memories with other students in the kitchen.

- Wine Tasting, Alentejo and Douro Valley — Portugal is a world-renowned wine producer, and when in the country of Port, you need to experience all the flavors of the wine from the best wine regions. You can go on wine tours and partake in wine tasting in Alentejo and the Douro Valley. You can also explore the plantations and vineyards or stay overnight at some accommodations to spend more time in the Portuguese wine country. Vinhos Verdes, another region to visit along the Rivers Minho and Douro, is a special place where you can taste what is known as "green wine" due to the land which is in the northwest of Portugal. The wine produced here is not green in color, but rather referred to as 'green' because it is farmed in the area Vinhos Verdes, which translates to

"Green Wines." You can taste and purchase all types of wine from rosé to white.

- Tavern hopping—the country of Portugal is big on taverns, known as *tascas* or *tasquinhas*. These establishments can be found across the country and are where locals and tourists alike gather to enjoy the Portuguese gastronomic culture. Taverns are usually locally run and serve inexpensive but large local dishes. Taverns are often small and hold traditional charm which make them intimate and quaint with no pretension and sometimes outdated decorations. The food at these taverns is usually served with local wines which only enhances the warm feeling in these friendly eateries.

- Boat tour on Tagus River, Lisbon—you can book a boat ride on the river for a sunset tour of the city. Some sites you will be able to spot on this tour are the Belém Tower, Lisbon Cathedral, and St. George's Castle. This is a great way to sightsee in Lisbon from a different viewpoint. Some cruises include wine and snacks in the tour, depending on which company and package you go with. No matter what time of day and the beverages you choose, the company you keep and traveling through

Lisbon on the River Tagus is a magnificent experience nonetheless.

- Toboggan ride, Monte to Fuchal—this is a unique and exhilarating ride to make your way from Funchal to Monte. The steep road that connects Funchal to Monte allows for a five-kilometer hilly road, and you can ride down this hill with a toboggan. An old-fashioned, two-seat toboggan is available to rent with the help of two men wearing rubber boots serving as your human brakes and guides. You can make your way down the path to Funchal in 10 minutes as you travel at the speed of 48 kilometers per hour. If you are looking for a thrill and would also like to explore Funchal, why not get there by toboggan?

- Michelin Star Restaurants—there are many Michelin star restaurants in Portugal, but one that offers delicious food with a rare experience is Blind, a dining experience that will awaken your taste buds. The idea is that you cannot see your food while you are eating and only rely on your other senses to appreciate the chef's culinary art made for you to enjoy. Cuisine: Mediterranean, European; Location: R. de Entreparedes 40, Porto.

- Tuk Tuk tours, Lisbon—you can explore the city of Lisbon on a special ride, a Tuk Tuk, which will allow you to have a personal experience in an open vehicle. This is a great way to take in all the sites as this vehicle travels at a slower speed and has no doors, which makes it perfect for viewing iconic buildings and streets with no rush. Not only is this a great way to see places of interest, but it is also just a special travel experience.

CONCLUSION

We have gone through the many exciting and historical attractions that Portugal has in store for its travelers like you. The European country has a perfect blend of medieval and contemporary buildings, cityscapes, as well as unspoiled beaches and mountainous regions. From the very first chapter of this guide to the last, we discussed the important information, processes, and steps that are required when planning your trip to Portugal. A holiday abroad should serve your best interests and you should be able to live out all your desires by scratching off all the items on your travel wishlist. In this guide, we looked at the many tricks you can try out to ensure that you enjoy your holiday in Portugal. We also discussed the possibilities of even moving to Portugal for a more long-term stay or even making it your forever home. Portugal is a perfect place to retire as it offers a great opportunity to live in a coastal climate for an affordable price. All these possibilities and the preparations needed for visiting or living in Portugal in the near future were discussed in this guide.

Portugal is a country with so much natural beauty and unobstructed views, but it also provides all the amenities and that hustle and bustle feeling in its cities, specifically Lisbon and Porto. Knowing what you want to do and where you want to go on your Portuguese trip will inspire you to learn and explore before you even get to Portugal. This informed adventurer spirit was encouraged in Chapter 1. Here, we learned about how to create an itinerary that fits your travel wishlist, your length of stay, and your budget. We also discussed smart, money-saving hacks to help you stick to your holiday budget while saving time and finding the most convenient travel options for your stay.

In Chapter 2, we moved on to the fun part, we discussed the many sights and natural treasures you can explore in Portugal. The country has so much history that has been preserved for centuries with old buildings like chapels and castles which are located among stunning seaside scapes or green backdrops. We quickly established the rare charm of Portugal, where the blend of grand buildings and nature is displayed, highlighting the age and history held in the country's walls and tall trees.

Chapter 3 focused on the essential parts of your fun-filled getaway, including food and accommodation. Again, we stuck to the vital factors of budgeting, convenience, and the varying preferences of different travelers. Some people might want to dine out at Michelin star restaurants and others may be more than happy to have an authentic Portuguese meal at a local tavern. A traveler with a big budget and desire for luxury might want to stay at one of the 5-star hotels we listed, while another could be looking for budget accommodation in a hostel or opt for a more authentic Portuguese living experience in a local's house in one of our listed homestays. No matter what type of traveler you are, we covered your bases for you.

Moving from holidaying in Portugal to settling in the country, Chapter 4 was an introduction to the journey of moving or retiring to the European coastal country. Portugal has seen a rise in expats who have chosen to make it their new home. The country has seen expats of all ages from different phases of life. It is very clear that Portugal has something special to offer for all its new inhabitants. In this chapter, we looked at the potential cities and towns that one could call their new home. We also compared the pros and cons of living and retiring in Portugal. While the lifestyle is laidback and affordable for a place that makes you feel like you are on holiday every day, there are procedures and precautions you would need to take before making the move. Not only is documentation and legal processing important, but so is the adjustment process involved in moving to Portugal, so this is why we touched on the Portuguese social life and norms.

Chapter 5 was a vital part of this guide as we went through the latest Covid-19 protocols as well as the Portuguese travel policies that need to be followed. Before you can land in Portugal, you need to know what is required of you and the steps you need to take to follow Portuguese Covid-19 policies to prevent the spread of the virus. While it can put a damper on your holiday mode, planning ahead and remaining informed about as much as possible when embarking on a trip abroad during a global pandemic is vital for your health and the safety of others. Being prepared and making wise choices can only save and help you in the long run as no one wants to be quarantined or ill on their holiday.

Lastly, we learned about some special self-guided tours and activities you can try out as you travel across the country. We discussed the brilliant gems of small towns and old villages as well as the popular festivals and tours you could take when moving from town to town and from north to south of the country. Depending on your interests, you could find yourself spending your day doing water sports in the Algarve, hiking in Madeira, or even going on wine tours in the Douro Valley. Whatever you are up for and wherever you are, Portugal can offer you a relaxing and reviving experience of a lifetime. All you need to do is make your move and take that leap by opening your mind to so many possibilities so that you can live your seaside dreams in the naturally beautiful and pristine country of Portugal.

REFERENCES

23 pro tips for saving money on travel. (2022). Travel Channel. https://www.travelchannel.com/interests/budget/articles/23-pro-tips-for-saving-money-on-travel

Accommodations in Portugal. (2022). Booking.com. https://www.booking.com/accommodation/country/pt.en-gb.html?aid=356980

Atlas Obscura. (2022a). *16 hidden gems to visit in Portugal*. Atlas Obscura. https://www.atlasobscura.com/lists/portugal-unique-places-to-visit

Atlas Obscura. (2022b). *Unusual attractions in Portugal*. Atlas Obscura. https://www.atlasobscura.com/things-to-do/portugal

Becca. (2022, February 27). *28 ways how to save money while traveling*. Halfhalftravel. https://www.halfhalftravel.com/travel-advice/ways-to-save-money-while-traveling.html

Bernhardt, P. (2020a, June 8). *20 best places to visit in Portugal*. Planet Ware. https://www.planetware.com/portugal/best-places-to-visit-in-portugal-p-1-22.htm

Bernhardt, P. (2020b, September 14). *22 top-rated tourist attractions in Portugal*. Planet Ware. https://www.planetware.com/tourist-attractions/portugal-p.htm

Best hidden gems in Portugal. (2022). European Best Destinations. https://www.europeanbestdestinations.com/destinations/portugal/best-hidden-gems-in-portugal/

Best natural attractions in Portugal. (2020). Inspirock. https://www.inspirock.com/natural-attractions-in-portugal

Best natural wonders in Portugal. (2022). Europe's Best Destinations. https://www.europeanbestdestinations.com/destinations/portugal/best-natural-wonders-in-portugal/

Brücker, A. (2018). *Lisbon cityscape sunset*. Unsplash. [Image]. https://unsplash.com/photos/X87yB-jvYHw

Covid-19 | measures implemented in Portugal. (2022, February 19). Visit Portugal.

https://www.visitportugal.com/en/content/covid-19-measures-implemented-portugal

Events and festivals in Portugal. (2022). Portugal.net. https://www.portugal.net/en/events-festivals-portugal/

Foodandroad. (2021, February 2). *5 food and wine experiences to try in Portugal*. Food 'N Road. https://foodandroad.com/food-travel-experiences-portugal/

Ghangas, S. (2021, November 30). *These 11 restaurants in Portugal will familiarise you with the country even more*. Travel Triangle. https://traveltriangle.com/blog/restaurants-in-portugal/

Holiday Parrots. (2021, April 3). *22 top-rated tourist attractions in Portugal*. Holiday Parrots. https://holidayparrots.com/tourist-attractions-portugal/

Kaharlytskyi, M. (2019). *Four shades of vine*. Unsplash. [Image]. https://unsplash.com/photos/3uJt73tr4hI

Lonely Planet. (2020, August 18). *Portugal's top 10 natural wonders*. Lonely Planet. https://www.lonelyplanet.com/articles/portugal-top-natural-wonders

Maunder, S. (2022, March 2). *How to retire in Portugal: Your top questions answered.* Expatica. https://www.expatica.com/pt/finance/retirement/retire-in-portugal-908573/

McKay, L. (2017). *Looking out over Alfama, Lisbon.* Unsplash. [Image]. https://unsplash.com/photos/VHWyqXsWHg0

Nomadic Matt. (2021, May 29). *18 easy steps planning your next trip.* Nomadic Matt's Travel Site. https://www.nomadicmatt.com/travel-blogs/planning-a-trip/

Pettit, S. (2022, March 3). *The best places to live in Portugal as an expat.* Expatica. https://www.expatica.com/pt/moving/location/best-places-in-portugal-105521/

Pires, M. (2021, September 21). *The 32 essential Lisbon restaurants* (R. Tonon, Ed.). Eater. https://www.eater.com/maps/best-lisbon-portugal-restaurants

Resende, R. (2018). *Group of people beside water.* Unsplash. [Image]. https://unsplash.com/photos/swivynstICo

Restaurants in Portugal. (2018). Travel + Leisure. https://www.travelandleisure.com/travel-guide/portugal/restaurants

Restaurants in Portugal. (2022). Tripadvisor.
https://www.tripadvisor.co.za/Restaurants-
g189100-Portugal.html

Retire in Portugal. (2022). International Living.
https://internationalliving.com/countries/portug
al/retire-in-portugal/

Rogala, B. (2018, December 25). *8 tips for planning an
international trip on a budget.* Outside Online.
https://www.outsideonline.com/adventure-
travel/advice/budget-international-travel-tips/

Sam, R. (2021). *Douro Valley - quinta de la rosa. Pinhão,
Portugal.* Unsplash. [Image].
https://unsplash.com/photos/53kK4Wmr4Cs

Sangster, R. (2017, December). *The checklist for budget
travel abroad.* Transitions Abroad.
https://www.transitionsabroad.com/publications
/magazine/0707/budget_travel_tips_for_checklist.
shtml

Santos, N. (2021, September 13). *The best destinations to
visit in Portugal.* Culture Trip.
https://theculturetrip.com/europe/portugal/artic
les/the-15-best-destinations-to-visit-in-portugal-in-
2017/

Self-guided tours & trips in Portugal. (2022). Tourradar.
https://www.tourradar.com/i/portugal-self-
guided

The complete guide to retiring in Portugal. (2022, March 1). Get Golden Visa. https://getgoldenvisa.com/retiring-in-portugal#:~:text=You%20need%20to%20apply%20for

The Portuguese lifestyle. (2021, September 24). Expat.com. https://www.expat.com/en/guide/europe/portugal/10782-lifestyle-in-portugal.html

Tiago. (2021, February 11). *Retire in Portugal and choose where to live in this amazing country.* Go to Portugal. https://gotoportugal.eu/en/retire-in-portugal/

touropia. (2021, September 25). *10 top tourist attractions in Portugal.* Touropia. https://www.touropia.com/tourist-attractions-in-portugal/

Viator. (2022). *Top Portugal dining experiences.* Viator. https://www.viator.com/en-ZA/Portugal-tours/Dining-Experiences/d63-g6-c20

Walking holidays in Portugal. (2020). Exodus Travels. https://www.exodustravels.com/il/portugal-holidays/walking

Where to go in portugal: 10 secret spots the locals love. (2022). Times Travel.

https://www.thetimes.co.uk/travel/destinations/
europe/portugal/secret-spots-locals-love

Yakiwchuk, L. (2021, June 23). *How to plan an
international trip: Practical tips for traveling abroad.*
Justin plus Lauren.
https://justinpluslauren.com/how-to-plan-an-
international-trip/